Post-Herald

g' Newspaper

ALABAMA: Cloudy, mild, showers.

FINAL EDITION

PRICE FIVE CENTS

PTEMBER 16, 1963

22 Pages In Two Sections

HURCH, KILLS 4

S RUSHED HER

*Birmingham suffered so many racially motivated bombings...
the city was nicknamed "Bombingham."*

Birmingham Sunday

LARRY DANE BRIMNER

CALKINS CREEK
HONESDALE, PENNSYLVANIA

Jacket Photos
(left) The thirty-inch-thick stone and brick foundation walls tumbled in when dynamite exploded outside the Sixteenth Street Baptist Church on September 15, 1963; (right) a new sanctuary rose from the rubble with a stained-glass window that was donated by the children of Wales in the United Kingdom.

Printed in China

Library of Congress Cataloging-in-Publication Data

Brimner, Larry Dane.
 Birmingham Sunday / Larry Dane Brimner. — 1st ed.
   p. cm.
 Includes bibliographical references.
 ISBN 978-1-59078-613-0 (hardcover : alk. paper)
 1. Birmingham (Ala.)—Race relations—History—20th century—Juvenile literature. 2. African Americans—Civil rights—Alabama—Birmingham—History—20th century—Juvenile literature. 3. African Americans—Crimes against—Alabama—Birmingham—History—20th century—Juvenile literature. 4. Ku Klux Klan (1915–)—Alabama—Birmingham—History—20th century—Juvenile literature. 5. Bombings—Alabama—Birmingham—History—20th century—Juvenile literature. 6. Hate crimes—Alabama—Birmingham—History—20th century—Juvenile literature. 7. Racism—Alabama—Birmingham—History—20th century—Juvenile literature. 8. Sixteenth Street Baptist Church (Birmingham, Ala.)—Juvenile literature. I. Title.
 F334.B69B75 2010
 323.1196'0730761781—dc22

                                    2009035716

CALKINS CREEK
An Imprint of Boyds Mills Press
815 Church Street
Honesdale, Pennsylvania 18431

First edition
The text of this book is set in Sabon.

10 9 8 7 6 5

To the memory of Cynthia Wesley,
Carole Robertson, Addie Mae Collins, Denise McNair,
Johnny Brown Robinson, Virgil Ware, and all the other
innocent victims in the ongoing struggle for human
rights in the United States and the world

—LDB

Trapped in the basement when dynamite exploded outside the Sixteenth Street Baptist Church on September 15, 1963 were: (top, left to right) Addie Mae Collins and Cynthia Wesley; (bottom, left to right) Carole Robertson and Denise McNair.

As SHE OFTEN DID,
FOURTEEN-YEAR-OLD ADDIE MAE COLLINS

walked the sixteen blocks to church on Sunday morning with her older sister, Janie, and younger sister, Sarah.

It was September 15, 1963.

Pretty, all dressed in white, the sisters began to toss Janie's purse back and forth along their way, playing a makeshift game of football. The walk usually took them fifteen or twenty minutes, but they were having such fun on that chilly, gray Alabama morning. By the time they reached Birmingham's Sixteenth Street Baptist Church, Sunday school was almost over. All three were sweaty, so they hurried down the stairs to the basement to freshen up in the women's bathroom.

As she left the bathroom minutes later, Janie cautioned her sisters not to dillydally, and she left for the main sanctuary. It was youth day at the church, and all the young people were to meet upstairs at 10:30.

At the Wesley home,

fourteen-year-old Cynthia was ready for church. When she got to the door, though, her mother gave her a disapproving look. Her sister, Shirley, related how their mother chided Cynthia: "Young lady . . . you just don't put your clothes on any way when you're going to church. . . ." Cynthia quickly adjusted her slip, which had been showing. Then she and her father left for church. They arrived at the Sixteenth Street Baptist Church before the start of Sunday school at 9:30.

Carole Robertson, also fourteen, was Cynthia's close friend. Driven by her father, Carole was already at church when Cynthia arrived. The girls went to their Sunday school class, but they were so excited about their youth day duties that at around ten minutes after ten they asked to be excused so they could freshen up for the service.

At about the same time, eleven-year-old Denise McNair got to church. She hurried to join her Sunday school class in the basement but asked to be excused minutes later. When Denise walked into the women's bathroom, Cynthia and Carole were fussing and primping. Sarah was washing her hands at the sink. The sash on Denise's dress had come undone, so she asked Addie Mae to retie the bow for her.

Suddenly, a blast ripped through the building. Windows shattered. And thirty-inch-thick stone and brick walls thundered. Reverend John Cross, the church pastor, said, "It sounded like the whole world was shaking, and the building, I thought, was going to collapse." The clock in the main worship hall froze at 10:22.

If a man say, I love God, and hateth his brother, he is a liar: for he that loveth not his brother whom he hath seen, how can he love God whom he hath not seen?
—1 John 4:20

The blast at the Sixteenth Street Baptist Church was caused by ten to nineteen sticks of dynamite that were placed under the church stairs just outside the women's bathroom. Leaving a gaping hole in the foundation and creating a deep crater in the basement, the blast buried the five young girls.

BROWN V. THE BOARD OF EDUCATION

In 1896, the United States Supreme Court upheld racial segregation as long as the separate facilities were equal. In 1954, the Court reversed that decision when it declared that separation based on race (color), by its very nature, was unequal. Although the 1896 ruling dealt with segregation on railway cars traveling within the state of Louisiana, the decision soon was applied to restaurants, public bathrooms, movie theaters, schools, and almost every other aspect of American life.

In 1951, Topeka's Negro children could enroll in only four of the city's twenty-two elementary schools. Recruited by the National Association for the Advancement of Colored People (NAACP), thirteen parents filed a legal challenge to the Topeka school board's policy of segregation on behalf of their twenty children. Eventually reaching the Supreme Court, the so-called Brown case—named for one of the parents—was combined with lawsuits from Delaware, South Carolina, Virginia, and Washington, D.C., because all were seeking the same outcome. Representing nearly two hundred plaintiffs, the Brown case successfully challenged racial segregation and paved the way for social reform and the civil rights movement.

The U.S. Supreme Court's separate-but-equal ruling of 1896 was applied to every aspect of life in the South, from jails (top) to movie theaters (right), from drinking fountains to public bathrooms.

BIRMINGHAM HAD BEEN ROCKED BY PROTESTS AND VIOLENCE THROUGHOUT 1963.

In 1954, the milestone United States Supreme Court decision in *Oliver L. Brown et al. versus the Board of Education of Topeka (Kansas)* outlawed racial segregation, or separation, in schools and other public places and ruled that integration should move forward with "deliberate speed." But Birmingham, like most other cities and towns in the South, was still very much divided into black and white. Separate black and white seating in movie houses. Separate black and white waiting areas at the bus depot. Separate black and white drinking fountains. Negroes were welcome to spend their money in white-owned department stores, but they were not allowed to use the fitting rooms, sit at the lunch counters, or use the bathrooms. Zoning restrictions prohibited blacks from living in many parts of the city. And black

children and white children attended separate schools. This practice of racial segregation was known as "Jim Crow," a phrase that originated from a popular nineteenth-century minstrel song performed by a white singer in blackface. Despite the *Brown* decision, white Southern politicians usually ran on the campaign promise to uphold and enforce these Jim Crow laws, and so in 1963 George C. Wallace, Alabama's newly elected governor, declared in his inaugural speech,

"[S]egregation today . . . segregation tomorrow . . . segregation forever."

George C. Wallace (right), Alabama's newly elected governor, gained national attention when he stood in the schoolhouse door in an attempt to block two Negroes, James Hood and Vivian Malone, from entering the University of Alabama.

Before the mid-1960s, segregation was part of the fabric of life in the United States, but nowhere was it more deeply entrenched than in the South. Following the Civil War and the South's defeat in 1865, many white Southerners were filled with fear, resentment, and hatred. Their agrarian way of life, which was borne on the backs of Negro slaves, had ended; their economy was devastated. Several Confederate veterans decided to take action. In 1866, they organized the Ku Klux Klan (KKK) to control the social, economic, and political lives of blacks. It quickly spread to communities large and small throughout the South and beyond.

In a rare 1923 photograph, hooded Ku Klux Klan members ride through the streets at night, on horses draped in white and hooves muffled, to intimidate those who do not agree with them.

An armed vigilante group, the KKK played on people's fears of a violent Negro uprising—retaliation for all the years of slavery and suffering. KKK members also took advantage of people's superstitions by wearing flowing white sheets and concealing their faces with white masks. Sometimes they draped their horses in white robes and muffled the horses' hooves. Riding at night, the disguised Klansmen were an elaborate and terrorizing performance of ghosts of Confederate soldiers returning from the battlefields. Yet their actions were anything but make-believe. Klansmen raided black homes, broke up black church meetings, and ran out of town anyone who tried to help blacks improve their lives. These patrols were usually enough to intimidate blacks—and any whites who supported them—into quiet submission. When they did not, the Klan turned to mob violence, often lynching, or hanging, those who dared to defy their notion of white supremacy.

Brown decision was thrust into a South shaped by Klan hatred. The first test of the decision came in 1956 in Alabama. Two years before *Brown* became law, Autherine Lucy was accepted to the University of Alabama in Tuscaloosa. She had dreamed of becoming a librarian. But once university officials realized that she was black, they told her it was against state law to admit her. With the help of the National Association for the Advancement of Colored People (NAACP), she sued the university, and in 1955 the Supreme Court ordered the university to admit her. In February 1956, Lucy enrolled, but on the third day of classes she was met by white students and Klan members hurling threats, racial slurs, eggs, and rocks. They waved Confederate flags. Lucy had to be escorted off the campus in a police car for her own protection. The university suspended her later that evening—citing safety as the main reason—and it later expelled her when she challenged its actions. Violence had won the day.

WALK FOR EQUALITY

On December 1, 1955, Rosa Parks (1913–2005), a forty-two-year-old seamstress, tested the legality of so-called "Jim Crow" segregation laws that required Negroes to sit in the back of buses. Working with the NAACP, she boarded a bus in Montgomery, Alabama, and refused to give up her seat to a standing white man. This act of defiance was met with a police arrest. The black community quickly galvanized to protest Mrs. Parks's arrest and the guilty verdict that followed. Negroes boycotted Montgomery's bus system. They walked to work, shared rides with friends who had automobiles, or took black-owned taxis rather than using the city's segregated buses. The Montgomery bus boycott strained the city's finances while the appeal of Mrs. Parks's guilty verdict worked its way through the legal system.

Rosa Parks, though, wasn't the first person to be prosecuted under Alabama's strict segregation laws. Countless men and women had taken stands against Jim Crow. Among them were four women in Montgomery: Aurelia S. Browder, Susie McDonald, fifteen-year-old Claudette Colvin, and Mary Louise Smith. In the months before Mrs. Parks's arrest, all four had faced discrimination on city buses, and they agreed to challenge the constitutionality of city and state bus segregation laws. In the case known as Browder v. Gayle (W. A. "Tacky" Gayle was the mayor of Montgomery), their attorneys—E. D. Nixon, Fred Gray, and Clifford Durr—filed suit in U.S. District Court claiming that the laws violated the U.S. Constitution. The court agreed, and its decision was affirmed by the Supreme Court in November 1956, thus making Jim Crow seating on buses illegal. The ruling reached Montgomery on December 20, and the bus boycott, after 381 days, ended in triumph the next day. Mrs. Parks is remembered as the mother of the civil rights movement for her act of civil disobedience and for inspiring the Montgomery bus boycott. It was the Browder ruling, however, that ended segregated seating on buses. Mrs. Parks's guilty verdict remained on Alabama's state criminal records until 2006 when the state legislature passed and Governor Bob Riley signed the Rosa Parks Act, which officially granted pardons to all those who had been convicted of violating the Jim Crow laws.

Autherine Lucy, with her attorneys, Thurgood Marshall (center) and Arthur Shores (right), leaving court after Lucy was expelled from the University of Alabama in February 1956.

The NAACP got its start in a little room of a New York City apartment in January 1909 at a meeting of writer William English Walling, Dr. Henry Moskowitz, and Mary White Ovington, a social reformer and writer. The three had been shocked by a race riot the previous summer in Springfield, Illinois, Abraham Lincoln's hometown. The exact cause of the riot is still subject of debate. Some historians believe it was the result of competition in a tight job market, while others maintain it was class warfare, with wealthier blacks as the main targets of hate by less fortunate whites. What is known is that an alleged attack of a white woman by a black man sparked the initial violence. The woman later admitted she'd lied, but on the evening of August 14, 1908, a mob of the city's white citizens began killing or wounding scores of colored people. The angry crowd drove thousands out of town. The riot raged for two days.

Walling, Moskowitz, and Ovington decided that it was time to take stock of the nation's progress on racial equality since the end of the Civil War. On February 12, the centennial of Lincoln's birth, they and more than thirty other concerned citizens issued a call for a national conference to discuss the state of race relations in the United States. Out of that conference, which was held in New York City on May 30, sprang the National Negro Committee. One year later, the small group officially changed its name to the National Association for the Advancement of Colored People. In the spirit of the abolitionists who wished to abolish slavery and make every person equal partners in a free society, the NAACP was charged with securing equality of opportunity and equal application of the law for every citizen, regardless of color.

University of Alabama students wipe their eyes after police blasted them with tear gas in an attempt to break up demonstrations against the enrollment of Autherine Lucy.

At the same time, in Alabama's capital, other challenges to Jim Crow were taking place. Rosa Parks and others were fighting segregated seating on Montgomery's city buses. The NAACP and prominent civil rights leaders were pushing to end Jim Crow segregation on as many different social levels and in as many different cities and towns as possible. And at every turn—in Georgia, Mississippi, Tennessee, Texas, Arkansas, Louisiana, North Carolina, Florida, Alabama, and other places—attempts to desegregate were met by outraged white citizenry and Klan reprisals.

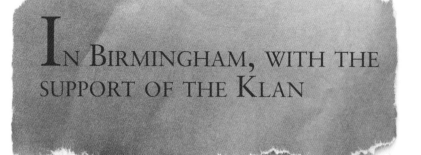

In Birmingham, with the support of the Klan

> *"the biggest thing that had happened to Negroes almost since emancipation."*

and by promising to uphold segregation, Theophilus Eugene "Bull" Connor (1897–1973) was elected Commissioner of Public Safety in 1937, an office he would hold off and on until 1963. In a city with a commission form of government, the post gave him unequaled power. He was head of both the police and fire departments, and he operated independently of Birmingham's two other commissioners. Throughout the 1940s, he ruled the city with an iron hand, often boasting that he knew how to keep Negroes in their place.

What Connor failed to anticipate, however, was the arrival of a black preacher named Fred Shuttlesworth (1922–), who believed that a minister's job didn't end with a Sunday sermon from the pulpit. It extended beyond his congregation's spiritual needs to include its social and civic well-being. From the time that Shuttlesworth came to Birmingham's Bethel Baptist Church—a black congregation— in 1953, he was speaking out for equality. For him, the 1954 *Brown* decision was "the biggest thing that had happened to Negroes almost since emancipation." It confirmed for him that segregation was wrong. But the decision also "resulted in hardening the attitude of the Southern states."

Birmingham police commissioner Eugene "Bull" Connor was a fiery segregationist who often claimed he knew how to keep Negroes in their place.

SHUTTLESWORTH TOOK THE HARDENING OF ATTITUDE AS A CHALLENGE.

Time and again, his Sunday sermons preached equal status with whites. A member of the NAACP, he took up its call for increased black voter registration almost every Sunday because he believed in the power of the vote to change the injustices that Negroes faced. He accompanied Autherine Lucy, an old friend, to the University of Alabama when she went to enroll in 1956— and two weeks later a brick was thrown through his parsonage window in Birmingham. The brick was Klan reprisal for his vocal support of integrated schools— and it was a warning.

In retaliation for the NAACP's role in the Lucy case and the Montgomery bus boycott, Alabama's attorney general outlawed the financially strapped organization in June 1956 when courts upheld the state's incorporation regulations, which required organizations operating within the state to be incorporated there. The NAACP was incorporated in New York. To skirt the Alabama law, Shuttlesworth promptly founded the Alabama Christian Movement for Human Rights (ACMHR). In Birmingham, the ACMHR took up the work of the NAACP, challenging segregation where the latter organization could not. Following the successful outcome of the Montgomery bus boycott, Shuttlesworth, as president of the ACMHR, sent Birmingham's commissioners an ultimatum on December 20 to either desegregate the city's buses or face a similar boycott. On Christmas night, the Klan bombed his home. The city's buses remained segregated, but Shuttlesworth saw his survival of the bomb blast as a sign from God that he was meant to lead Birmingham's movement for civil rights. And lead a movement is just what

On Christmas night, the Ku Klux Klan dynamited the home of Reverend Fred L. Shuttlesworth for his outspoken support of school integration and racial equality. Shuttlesworth interpreted his survival of the blast as a sign from God that he was meant to lead Birmingham's struggle for civil rights.

You may knock me down
I'll rise again
I'm washed by the blood of the Lamb
I fight you with my sword and shield
I'm washed by the blood of the Lamb

to safety and sped him to the hospital. The doctor was certain that Shuttlesworth had had a concussion, but he could find no evidence of one. His sense of humor still intact, Shuttlesworth explained it to the doctor this way: "Well . . . the Lord knew I lived in a hard town so he gave me a hard skull."

he did. He transformed Bethel Baptist Church from a house of God to a center of civil rights action.

Shuttlesworth was more than a cheerleader urging his congregation and followers to action. For every act he requested of them, he was out front, leading the way. Branded a rabble-rouser by Connor and believing that ministers should set an example, Shuttlesworth and his followers rode Birmingham's buses and sat up front, ignoring the segregated seating signs in late December. In March 1957, he and his wife, Ruby, sat in the white seating area at the Greyhound bus station, where they were met by the threats and taunts of a group of Klansmen. Although they were not attacked, a white supporter *was* beaten. In September, Shuttlesworth notified the police department that he would attempt to enroll his daughters, Pat and Ricky, in Birmingham's all-white Phillips High School. He requested police protection. Instead, Connor's police department notified the Klan, whose members were waiting for them and beat Shuttlesworth almost unconscious. An ACMHR supporter who had driven Shuttlesworth, Ruby, and their daughters to the school that morning pulled him

As he promised city commissioners he'd do if buses were not integrated by December 26, 1956, Shuttlesworth (wearing a hat) and an unidentified ACMHR supporter violated Jim Crow seating—beginning the day after the Shuttlesworth home was bombed.

In 1955, Martin Luther King, Jr., was a young minister new to both Montgomery, Alabama, and to Dexter Avenue Baptist Church, where he was pastor. He came to prominence leading that city's bus boycott of 1955–1956 in protest of the arrest of Rosa Parks, a Negro woman who had refused to give up her seat to a white passenger as custom and the law dictated. Following the success of the boycott, King was elected president of the Southern Christian Leadership Conference, an organization formed to bring an end to segregation laws and practices throughout the United States. For his nonviolent efforts to further racial equality, he was awarded the Nobel Peace Prize in 1964. On the evening of April 4, 1968, while in Memphis, Tennessee, to lend his support to striking sanitation workers, he was assassinated.

We want no cowards in our band
That will their colors fly
We call for valiant-hearted men
That are not afraid to die

A HARD TOWN. BIRMINGHAM WAS THAT, AND MORE.

Beginning in the late 1940s, Birmingham suffered so many racially motivated bombings—more than forty—that the city was nicknamed "Bombingham." Explosions were so common in one black neighborhood that it was commonly known as "Dynamite Hill." The Birmingham police department was riddled with Klan members and rarely investigated the bombings. Not surprisingly, none of the bombings was ever solved.

Ever since the Montgomery bus boycott, Shuttlesworth had urged Dr. Martin Luther King, Jr. (1929–1968), to shine the national spotlight on Birmingham through his organization, the Southern Christian Leadership Conference (SCLC). The SCLC had been founded in 1957 following the Montgomery bus boycott to continue protests of racial segregation throughout the South and beyond. Shuttlesworth believed that if King could desegregate Birmingham, the rest of the nation would follow. King was noncommittal, so Shuttlesworth and a small band of ACMHR loyalists continued their own protests of unequal treatment. These actions prompted Howard K. Smith, a CBS newsman who was in town to film *Who Speaks for Birmingham?*, a documentary, to call Shuttlesworth "the Negro feared most by the White Citizens of Birmingham."

Children learned racial hatred early in life. Here, Klan members are shown at a rally with their children in full regalia beside them.

IT WAS EASY TO SEE WHY SHUTTLESWORTH WAS FEARED BY RACISTS.

He refused to cower in the shadow of Klan violence, and he continued to use his pulpit as a soapbox to challenge injustice. Some of his followers said he was so fearless that they suspected he was a little crazy.

Crazy or not, Shuttlesworth continued to agitate for equality.

On Sunday, May 14, 1961, Freedom Riders were rolling through the South to dramatize the persistent use of segregated seating on interstate buses even though it was illegal. A racially mixed group of young people and retirees, both men and women, the Freedom Riders were led by the Congress of Racial Equality (CORE) and its cofounder James Farmer (1920–1999). Shuttlesworth prayed with his congregation for their safe journey to Birmingham, but he also anticipated Klan trouble. He contacted Connor, giving him the Freedom

THE CONGRESS OF RACIAL EQUALITY
The Congress of Racial Equality was founded in 1942 as the Committee of Racial Equality by a mixed-race group of students and activists, including James Farmer. A pacifist organization, it sought to bring about racial harmony and to change racist attitudes through Mahatma Gandhi's methods of nonviolent resistance.

Riders' expected arrival time and requesting that the police department provide them with protection.

When the buses—one Greyhound and one Trailways—arrived in Anniston, Alabama, an angry mob slashed the tires on the Greyhound bus to disable it and then set fire to it. As the Freedom Riders emerged choking and coughing from the bus, racists beat them with bats, clubs, bottles, and pipes. When the Trailways bus pulled in about an hour later, its passengers were also assaulted but the bus wasn't disabled, and its riders were able to continue on to Birmingham, where their experience was no less horrifying.

Connor had passed on Shuttlesworth's information about the Freedom Riders' expected arrival time to the Klan, telling them that he wanted these outsiders beaten—and beaten badly. And he promised to delay police response by fifteen minutes to give them time to do it. When the police finally came to the bus depot, the melee was over and the segregationists had fled.

The Freedom Riders met with violence when their buses rolled into Anniston, Alabama, in May 1961. The events in Anniston ended CORE's participation in the Freedom Rides, but its efforts were soon picked up by SNCC, the Student Nonviolent Coordinating Committee.

When Shuttlesworth heard about the attack, he made sure that shelter and medical aid were given to the Freedom Riders. He organized a caravan to travel to Anniston, despite the danger, to transport those stranded there to his Birmingham home.

For CORE, the violence had been too great, and the first Freedom Ride of the 1960s ended with the clashes in Anniston and Birmingham. The Freedom Riders were unable to find a bus company or any drivers willing to take them from Birmingham to New Orleans, their original destination, so several people flew to that Gulf Coast city. Others returned home. Even so, the Freedom Rides continued throughout 1961 as students from Nashville, Tennessee, and the Student Nonviolent Coordinating Committee—a group organized at Shaw University in Raleigh, North Carolina, to coordinate and publicize sit-ins—took up the effort, determined to prove that violence could not stop social justice.

For his part, Shuttlesworth continued to fight Birmingham's entrenched racial attitudes. The very next spring, Shuttlesworth and the ACMHR began a selective-buying campaign. They urged Negroes to make purchases only from stores that supported equal hiring. They petitioned city government to hire black police officers, open up civil service employment to blacks, and desegregate the parks. Birmingham's commissioners turned a deaf ear to these requests, and when they did, Shuttlesworth brought lawsuits against the city. Connor, however, was rigid in his support of segregation. He went so far as to threaten to close the city's parks rather than integrate them, and close them he did.

In the fall of 1962, King finally agreed to bring the SCLC to Birmingham. And as Shuttlesworth predicted,

the national spotlight shone on the city—but briefly. The next spring, Albert Boutwell became mayor of Birmingham in a shake-up at city hall. Many middle-class blacks—the professionals and business leaders who had made money by serving the Negro community—thought that Boutwell might in time bring about change by hiring blacks to work on the police force and in city government. They took a wait-and-see attitude. They urged Shuttlesworth and King, whose supporters were primarily poor and working-class blacks, to do the same. Shuttlesworth ignored them, while King told them that it was always time to do what is right. The new mayor, although not as vehement as Connor about segregation, was a segregationist nonetheless, and he knew his constituency. Conditions failed to improve for Birmingham's Negroes.

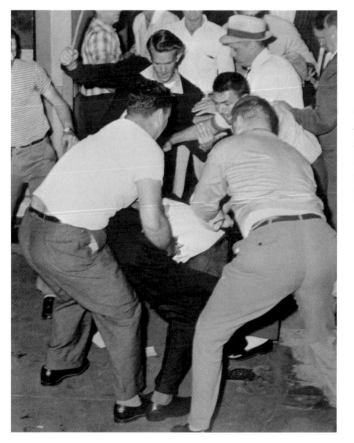

Freedom Rider James A. Peck is attacked and beaten by a white mob at the Birmingham bus depot.

IN EARLY APRIL 1963,

Shuttlesworth and the ACMHR encouraged students from local Miles College to sit in at five Birmingham department-store lunch counters. At first successful at focusing national attention on the unequal treatment of blacks in Birmingham, the sit-ins eventually fizzled when stores simply closed their lunch counters. Then on April 6, Shuttlesworth led the first joint ACMHR-SCLC protest march—coded "Project C" (for "confrontation")—of some forty or so demonstrators from the Sixteenth Street Baptist Church toward nearby city hall. The church was one of the largest in the city. It had the space to accommodate large

numbers of people at mass meetings and training sessions for nonviolent resistance. Even more important was its location—mere blocks from city hall.

After walking three blocks, Shuttlesworth's little group was stopped by chief of police Jamie Moore and Commissioner Connor. Shuttlesworth and his followers were told to turn back. Instead, they knelt in prayer and were arrested for unlawful parading.

The next day, ministers John Porter and Nelson H. Smith, Jr., joined Reverend Alfred D. King, Martin Luther King's brother and a local Baptist preacher, to lead another protest march to city hall. Spectators gathered along the sidewalks to watch the march, but this time, violence erupted. Unlike the marchers, the Negro spectators were untrained in the methods of nonviolence. They clashed with police over a new Connor tactic: the use of dogs to control the protesters. Photographs of police dogs going after Ullman High School sophomore Walter Gadsden, a bystander who had gone downtown only to see Martin Luther King, were published in newspapers around

(top) When Walter Gadsden was "attacked" by Connor's dogs and the image was published in newspapers around the world, it helped transform public opinion in 1963, although today there is some controversy as to whether he was being attacked. (bottom) Sit-ins by local college students soon fizzled when the department stores simply closed their lunch counters.

Reverend Dr. Martin Luther King, Jr., (right) and Reverend Ralph Abernathy led demonstrators from the Sixteenth Street Baptist Church toward Birmingham's city hall.

We shall overcome,
we shall overcome
We shall overcome some day
Oh, deep in my heart,
I do believe
We shall overcome some day

the globe. The event helped to transform public opinion about the plight of Negroes in the South. Birmingham's elite, middle-class blacks no longer had the luxury to wait and see. They, too, now endorsed the protests, even if they did not participate in them.

On Good Friday, April 12, the big three—Shuttlesworth, King, and Ralph Abernathy (1926–1990), one of King's advisers—led some fifty protesters toward city hall from the Sixteenth Street Baptist Church. A crowd of five hundred to one thousand onlookers filled the street behind them. Along the way, Shuttlesworth peeled off from the march, because their plan was to avoid having all three leaders in jail at the same time. King and Abernathy were met by Connor's police force and arrested. Later in the day, Shuttlesworth also was arrested.

After walking a few short blocks, King was arrested and taken to the Birmingham jail.

WHILE IN JAIL, KING READ

an ad in the city's white-owned newspaper, the *Birmingham News*, that called him a troublemaker and criticized the timing and methods of the protests. The ad had been taken out by eight of the city's white clergymen. King responded to the ministers in the margins of the newspaper, on toilet paper, and on any other scraps of paper he could find. These bits and pieces of paper were smuggled out of jail by his lawyers and later published as "Letter from Birmingham Jail." In his essay, King took to task these ministers and other moderate conservatives—the very people who urged blacks to take a patient course in their quest for freedom and equality. He laid at their feet the responsibility for the continuing second-class treatment of Birmingham's Negroes.

With the Birmingham campaign's big three in jail, more protesters took to the streets in the days that followed. Then, interest in protesting began to wane as Birmingham's black citizens took to heart threats of job loss and Klan violence. National television crews and newspaper reporters packed up, moving on to the next crisis. Even the local black-owned newspaper, the *Birmingham World*, denounced the demonstrations and its leaders, especially Shuttlesworth and King. The leaders knew that they had to come up with an idea that would grab the nation's attention, or risk losing its interest entirely—and with it, the campaign to desegregate Birmingham.

As King sat in jail, he formed his reply to eight white clergymen who called him a troublemaker for stirring up Negro anger and emotions in Birmingham. He responded with his "Letter from Birmingham Jail."

THE IDEA TO USE JUNIOR AND SENIOR HIGH-SCHOOL STUDENTS

as demonstrators came primarily from James Bevel (1936–2008), the SCLC's twenty-six-year-old director of Direct Action and Nonviolent Education. Young people were free of the financial responsibilities that made their parents more cautious about participating in protests. Shuttlesworth and others warmed to the idea, but King, who was released from jail on April 22, was reluctant. He worried about appearances. It might turn supporters against the civil rights movement—especially if any of the children were injured. The black middle class was shocked at the idea and dead set against any plans to implement it.

While King struggled to reach his decision, Bevel took action. He enlisted the help of high-school big shots, church youth leaders, and two WENN radio disc jockeys to recruit young people through a whisper campaign about nonviolence workshops and rallies at the Sixteenth Street Baptist Church. The idea was to make these youths think they were doing something half sneaky in the fight for freedom.

On May 2—Bevel called it D-Day—things heated up when, at noon, one of the WENN disc jockeys told kids that there was going to be a party at the park and that they should bring their toothbrushes. The "party" was a demonstration. The "park" was Kelly Ingram Park, which

Reverend James Bevel addresses a mass meeting at Sixteenth Street Baptist Church. The idea to use children in the fight for equality came primarily from him.

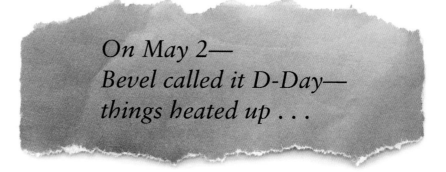

*On May 2—
Bevel called it D-Day—
things heated up . . .*

(top right) Connor ordered the use of fire hoses on young demonstrators when the children's crusade began. (bottom right) Children and teens proudly marched to the police wagons to be taken to jail.

. . . there was going to be a party at the park and that they should bring their toothbrushes.

lay diagonally across from the Sixteenth Street Baptist Church and was the line of demarcation between black and white Birmingham. That they should bring their "toothbrushes" meant they'd be filling Birmingham's jails.

The children's crusade began when hundreds of young people left school that Thursday. School administrators locked the doors and gates to try to prevent a mass exodus from the schools, but young people scurried over the fences anyway. Teachers, who would have lost their jobs had they spoken in favor of integration, turned their backs to their classes and children climbed out windows. Sixteenth Street Baptist Church filled with young people, each arriving group shouting out the name of its school. Then they poured into Kelly Ingram Park, and Connor brought out the dogs. The police wagons began to fill. Then wave after wave of youthful protesters arrived on the scene, and Connor called for fire trucks with high-pressure hoses—blasting water so powerful it could take the bark off trees—to be turned on the young demonstrators. By nightfall, more than one thousand teenagers sat in Birmingham's jails. And once again, Birmingham was in the headlines.

At first, Negroes were outraged

at black leaders who had encouraged their children to participate in the D-Day demonstrations. But when Connor ordered the use of dogs and hoses on their children, they directed their anger at him. It didn't take King long to realize that the energy of these youths was an asset to capturing the nation's attention, turning anger into protest, and winning the fight for racial equality. Events having made his decision for him, King endorsed the young people's demonstrations and told reporters at a news conference that they would continue until equality was won in Birmingham.

When Birmingham's jails filled to capacity, young demonstrators were housed at the state fairgrounds.

In the days that followed, the demonstrations grew. The violence grew. Before the children's crusade, Shuttlesworth had relied on only a handful of people to protest with him. The day King went to jail, he was arrested with only fifty or so other protesters. Now parents rallied alongside their abused children. They stood firm with Shuttlesworth and King.

By the time King called for an end to the demonstrations, the jails were overflowing. Scaling back the campaign's original demands for full equality, he negotiated a compromise—which some disagreed with—that included a promise from white business leaders, but no timeline, to desegregate lunch counters, drinking fountains, and bathrooms and an agreement to hire more black clerks in department stores. The compromise was announced on May 10, and the next night KKK bombs exploded at the black-owned A. G. Gaston Motel, where King lodged, and at the home of King's brother. Frustrated by the lack of gains and the continued abuse, rioters spilled into the streets, and President John F. Kennedy (1917–1963) ordered National Guard troops in Alabama to be on standby as an uneasy calm settled over Birmingham.

Reverend James Bevel uses a bull horn in an attempt to disperse a crowd of demonstrators on May 4, 1963.

IN THE MONTHS THAT FOLLOWED,

more bombs were set off in black neighborhoods—even as church rallies and demonstrations in Birmingham dwindled, even as a quarter million people marched on Washington, D.C., for jobs and freedom.

Then, life in the South began to undergo change. On September 4, 1963, for the first time, Birmingham

As Connor urged, white students stayed out of school in September 1963 and jeered from across the street as two black students were integrated into Birmingham's West End High School.

complied with a federal court order and reluctantly opened the doors at some of its white schools to black students. Members of the Klan and the National States Rights Party (NSRP) were filled with rage. The NSRP was a conservative political group founded in 1958 upon racism, with blacks and Jews as its main targets of hate. These two groups threatened violence and protested with placards even as Negro children were escorted through schoolhouse doorways.

Reverend Fred L. Shuttlesworth (foreground) accompanied James Armstrong (in dark suit, center) and his two sons into an all-white Birmingham school on September 1, 1963.

IT WAS MERE DAYS AFTER BIRMINGHAM'S COMPLIANCE

with the ordered school desegregation that the sun rose on September 15, 1963, bringing with it the first sweet hint of fall. It was youth day at the Sixteenth Street Baptist Church—the church Fred Shuttlesworth and Martin Luther King, Jr., had used the previous spring to organize and train protesters in the methods of nonviolent direct action for the Birmingham campaign. Young members of the church had a special role to play in the eleven o'clock worship service. Dressed in their Sunday best, some would be ushers, while others would sing in the choir or play the piano. After the day's Sunday school lesson, "The Love That Forgives," had been taught, all the young people were to meet upstairs in the sanctuary at ten thirty.

Cynthia Wesley, Carole Robertson, Addie Mae Collins and her sister Sarah, and Denise McNair were downstairs in the women's bathroom taking care of last-minute fixes to their hair and clothing before joining their friends upstairs. They wanted to look their best for their youth day duties. Suddenly, at 10:22, a dynamite blast rocked the building. Stained-glass windows shattered. And thirty-inch-thick stone and brick walls thundered, tumbling in on the five young girls.

So intense was the blast that it blew a passing motorist right out of his car. Across the street from the church, a man who was using a public telephone was whooshed into a neighborhood business. When he came to rest, the receiver was still in his hand.

Suddenly, at 10:22, a dynamite blast rocked the building.

Automobiles that were parked on the street beside the Sixteenth Street Baptist Church were blown four feet by the September 15 blast.

So intense was the blast that it blew a passing motorist right out of his car.

31

THE BLAST BROUGHT A QUICK REACTION

as angry, frustrated mobs surged into the streets. The wails of ambulance sirens were punctuated by the screams and accusations of rioters. The crowd was so large, said Reverend John Cross, that "it was making it almost impossible to do anything constructive . . . making threats against the police and if not threats, then verbally abusing them, accusing them." He got on a bullhorn and "started telling people the best thing that they could do was to vacate the premises and give the police and . . . [rescue workers] room to work." He promised them that whoever was responsible would "be brought to justice."

Cross not only wanted to expedite rescue efforts, but he also feared that there might be another blast. "This was the standard procedure, that they [the Klan] would have a blast to try to draw a crowd and another blast would go off, once the crowd got there."

When rescue workers began digging through the rubble and debris, they found the first body buried less than two feet down. Then the others came, one by one. "[T]hey were all on top of each other," Cross said, "as if they had hugged each other."

The next day, the *Birmingham Post-Herald* headline blared "BOMB BLAST KILLS 4 CHILDREN, INJURES 17 AT CHURCH HERE." The deaths of the four girls—Cynthia, Carole, Addie Mae, and Denise—had marked the first fatalities in more than forty unsolved bombing incidents in the city. Some say Sarah was the lucky one. She was blinded in one eye but escaped the blast with her life—and a lifetime of memories of that nightmarish morning.

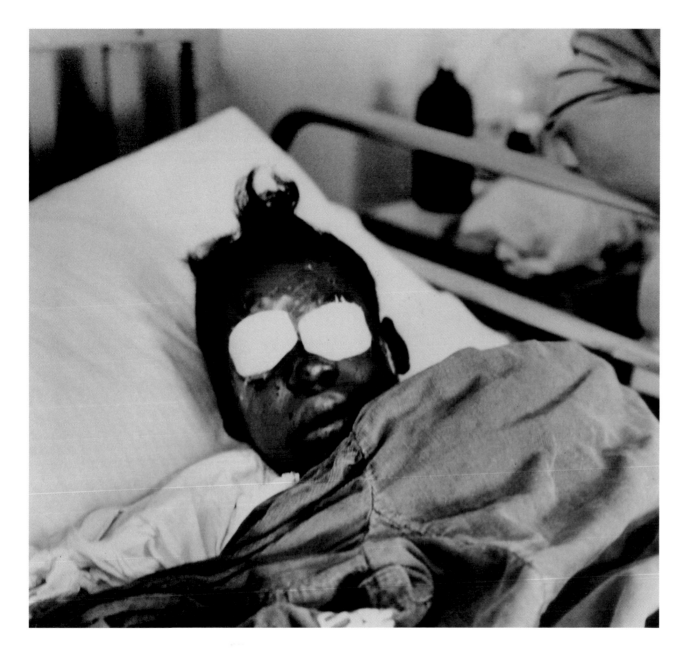

Sarah Collins, Addie Mae's twelve-year-old sister, survived the dynamite explosion with glass embedded in her eyes. The blast killed her sister and three other young girls.

On Birmingham Sunday the blood ran like wine,
And the choirs kept singing of Freedom.

CYNTHIA D. MORRIS WESLEY
(1949–1963)

Cynthia D. Morris Wesley was doted on by two families, her birth family and the family that raised her. Born April 30, 1949, she was one of eight children born into poverty. Estelle Morris, Cynthia's birth mother, wanted what was best for her daughter. She agreed to let Claude Wesley, a grade-school principal, and his wife, Gertrude, a nursery-school teacher, raise Cynthia as their own child. At six years of age, Cynthia suddenly brought life and laughter to the protective, childless Wesley home on Dynamite Hill.

A member of the Sixteenth Street Baptist Church's youth choir, Cynthia was a petite girl who made friends easily. "She would have little lawn parties," recalled Gerald Colbert, a childhood neighbor, and she often enjoyed entertaining her friends to the musical sounds of the Temptations and the Supremes. She took dance and music lessons, and played the saxophone in the band at Ullman High School, where she was an honor student.

She seemed never to forget her early childhood of hand-me-downs by helping those who were less fortunate. She saved her old music books for students who might not have been able to afford them. Friends said that if she had a dime, she would give it up to anybody who needed it. Dr. Freeman Hrabowski, III, a childhood friend, described Cynthia this way: "She was caring. . . . I was a fat little young boy. So some people didn't want to be bothered with me. Cynthia would be bothered with me . . . and be nice to me as a human being." Friends who knew her best have no doubt that, had she lived, she would have made it her life's work to help others.

"She would have little lawn parties."

CAROLE ROSAMOND ROBERTSON
(1949–1963)

Carole Rosamond Robertson was the third child of Alvin and Alpha Robertson. She was born on April 24, 1949. Her father was a band master at an elementary school and her mother, a librarian. She was little sister to Dianne and Alvin and was raised in a nurturing home that was full of love, good people, and good food. Like children everywhere, she had dreams. Hers, had she lived, was to teach history.

Carole was a typical teenager. Her childhood friend, Carolyn Lee Brown, recalled that "Carole was a very giving, outgoing person." She was bright and talented, loved to read, and made straight A's at Parker High School. On Saturday afternoons she toted her black patent-leather tap shoes and pink ballet slippers to dance lessons at the Smithfield Recreation Center. (Smithfield was a community of Negro professionals, the elite of black Birmingham.) Her life revolved around school, church, and family, and she rarely experienced an idle minute, belonging to Troop 264 of the Girl Scouts; the high school's marching band, choir, and science club; and Jack and Jill of America—a national organization that was founded to provide social, cultural, and recreational activities for children. She moved fast, as if to jam as much into her life as she could. "She played clarinet in the band," said her mother. "She was supposed to play her first game. That Monday night, after they were . . . After the bombing, they were . . . the band was supposed to play." In the weeks before the bombing, she was excited about attending a meeting of the newly formed Friendship and Action Committee—a local, grass-roots organization of black and white women that sprang out of the school desegregation orders. The group's purpose was to challenge Birmingham's rampant racism by letting the children of the city get to know each other.

"Carole was a very giving, outgoing person."

ADDIE MAE COLLINS
(1949–1963)

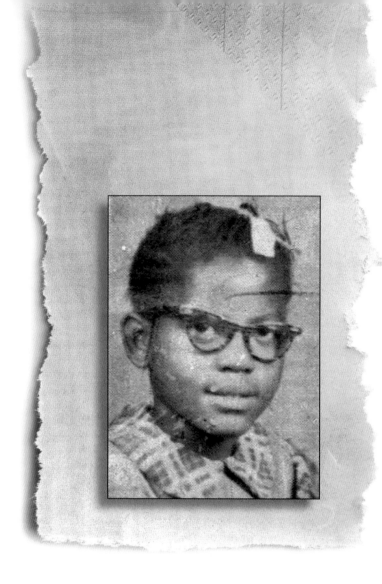

Reminiscing over happier times, Janie Gaines reflected on the younger sister she lost in the Sixteenth Street Baptist Church bombing. "To know Addie is to love Addie," she said of the Hill Elementary School eighth-grader. Addie Mae Collins was born on April 18, 1949, and she was a girl who loved playing games with her sisters. When disagreements erupted, she was the family peacemaker. "She was just . . . a sweet peaceful girl."

The seventh of eight children, Addie Mae was the daughter of Oscar and Alice Collins. Although the family lacked the material things that other members of the Sixteenth Street Baptist Church had, Janie believed her shy sister might have one day become a social worker, child care worker, or even a teacher. Addie Mae loved people and wanted to make everyone around her happy.

"She was just . . . a sweet peaceful girl."

CAROL DENISE MCNAIR
(1951–1963)

Carol Denise McNair was an advocate for the downtrodden and a champion for the disadvantaged—even at the age of eleven. When friends invited her to join a club but planned to exclude another friend because they doubted the child would be able to afford the nickel for membership, Denise didn't think it was fair. She offered to pay the nickel for her less fortunate friend. When she learned about an organization called the Muscular Dystrophy Association, which helped people stricken with the disease, she organized a neighborhood fund-raiser.

Born November 17, 1951, the Center Street School seventh-grader enjoyed putting on shows for friends and family members. Sometimes Denise would make a grand, flourishing entrance from behind the living-room curtains. Although her parents protected and isolated her as much as possible from the harsh realities of Birmingham's segregation, she heard about the children's crusade and wanted to participate. Her mother and her mother's cousin told her that she was too little. Disappointed, Denise looked at them for a moment. Then, according to her mother, and right in character, she said, "'You're not too little [too young].'" For Mrs. McNair, it was a painful charge that adults should have been at the forefront of protest instead of children.

"'You're not too little [too young].'"

JOHNNY BROWN ROBINSON
(1947–1963)

More lives would be claimed on Birmingham Sunday. After the blast at the Sixteenth Street Baptist Church—which investigators said was caused by ten to nineteen sticks of dynamite placed under the church's back stairs just outside the women's bathroom—chaos erupted in the streets. The first time bomb blasts touched off mass rioting was in the spring following the bombings of the A. G. Gaston Motel and of A. D. King's house. Once again, to vent their frustration and anguish, thousands of people poured into the area around the church and began throwing rocks and bricks at passing cars driven by white spectators. Seven hours after the church blast, one of those people in the street—Johnny Brown Robinson, sixteen—was shot in the back by police. The officer said that Johnny had been throwing rocks and ran, refusing to halt when ordered. The officer said he fired over Johnny's head, but the wound was fatal. Birmingham Sunday claimed its fifth victim.

VIRGIL WARE
(1950–1963)

James and Virgil Ware were going to see an uncle about a bicycle. The two had taken James's bike. Since he was bigger and older at sixteen, James pedaled. Thirteen-year-old Virgil perched on the handlebars. They wanted another bike so the two of them could deliver newspapers and save money to buy a car. The unrest that had rocked Birmingham for so long rarely touched the Wares. A mining family, they lived in an all-black suburb and seldom saw white folk. The brothers were unaware that there had been trouble that morning at the Sixteenth Street Baptist Church.

After learning that Virgil's bike wasn't yet ready, the two turned back toward home. As they sailed down a country road, two sixteen-year-old white youths—Michael Lee Farley and Larry Joe Sims—hurtled toward them on a small, red motorbike, its forty-cent Confederate flag fluttering proudly. The two white youths, both Eagle Scouts, had been fired up at a Klan-affiliated segregationist rally, and as they sped away from the meeting, Farley gave Sims his revolver to hold. The Eagle Scouts claimed that they thought the two black youths on the bicycle had rocks and were going to throw them. James disputed that, saying, "No we didn't have anything. You know he [Virgil] had both his hands on the handlebars and it took all I could for pedaling so we didn't have nothing." When the Eagle Scouts passed James and Virgil, Farley told Sims to shoot. Sims pulled the revolver out of his pocket, closed his eyes, and fired. *Pop! Pop!* Virgil fell off the handlebars to the ground.

"[W]ow, I'm shot," Virgil said, as James recounted the incident years later. Two bullets had struck Virgil's cheek and chest. He was the sixth and final black child to be killed that Birmingham Sunday.

JUSTICE WAS HARD TO FIND

"Well, it wasn't right."

in an environment that was corrupt, unjust, and flawed. But Farley and Sims were arrested the next day and charged with murder. Farley, who pled guilty, got probation. An all-white jury, however, convicted Sims, the shooter, on a lesser charge of manslaughter. The white judge, Wallace Gibson, sentenced him to six months in a juvenile facility, but then reduced the sentence to probation. Judge Gibson scolded both boys on their lapse in judgment. Was it justice? James Ware said, "Well, it wasn't right." Then, almost as an afterthought, he added, "To tell you the truth I didn't even expect them to catch them." In Bull Connor's Birmingham, crimes against Negroes usually went unsolved and unpunished. At least this crime had been solved.

The investigation into the Sixteenth Street Baptist Church bombing, however, seemed to go the way of most investigations into crimes against Negroes. Over the protestations of Alabama's governor, George Wallace, and Birmingham police, the Kennedy administration immediately sent agents from the Federal Bureau of Investigation (FBI) to lead the probe into the crime. But Governor Wallace resented the outside interference. He was determined that his people would solve it. The three investigating agencies—Alabama's state police, Birmingham police, and the FBI—did not cooperate with each other in their investigations. Then on September 29, Wallace made a hurried flight back from Florida to announce that his state investigators had made a break in the case. "We certainly beat the Kennedy crowd to the punch," he boasted.

*"We certainly beat the
Kennedy crowd to the punch."*

*The rebuilding of the
Sixteenth Street Baptist
Church began almost
immediately, and today
it is considered one of
the sacred places on the
civil rights trail.*

The next day, the state police arrested Robert Chambliss
and Charles Cagle. A couple of days later, they arrested John
Hall. All three men had been identified by the FBI as being
of interest and were under investigation, but the FBI didn't
believe there was enough evidence yet to make a case against
them. It was thought that their arrests at this early stage in
the investigation would taint the FBI's efforts to bring them to
justice. In the end, the FBI was correct. The three men were not
charged in the bombing of the church; rather, they were charged
with the misdemeanor crime of illegally possessing dynamite.
They were fined one hundred dollars each and received 180-day
jail sentences, which were suspended. And justice was delayed.

Fourteen years after the Sixteenth Street Baptist Church bombing, William J. Baxley, Alabama's attorney general, vowed to bring those responsible to justice.

and investigation had identified four serious suspects— Robert E. Chambliss, Bobby Frank Cherry, Herman Frank Cash, and Thomas E. Blanton, Jr., all KKK members—in the church bombing case. Although the FBI was convinced that other Klansmen knew about the plans to bomb the church, it was fairly certain that these four had played the major roles. Yet, it failed to bring charges against any of the men. Many speculated that FBI director J. Edgar Hoover (1895–1972) blocked prosecution because of his personal prejudice against blacks, especially Martin Luther King, Jr. The FBI, however, said that he wished to prevent leaks of information, since many among Alabama's law enforcement agencies were known to be allied with the KKK. There was also doubt that the evidence was substantial enough to win a case in what was then a white-controlled Birmingham. Also, in the 1960s, information from FBI surveillance was inadmissible in court, and the agency's key witnesses had refused to testify because of feared Klan retaliation.

It would take fourteen years and a young, energetic, determined attorney to prosecute the case. William J. Baxley (1941–), Alabama's attorney general, vowed to bring those

"'Let them wait till after Sunday morning. They will beg us to segregate.'"

Robert Chambliss, shown here in his mug shot, was convicted of murder in 1977 and died in prison in 1985.

responsible to trial. His efforts were hampered by the FBI, which at first refused to share its information in the case. "I am not so sure that it wasn't more of a bureaucratic mess than a deliberate effort to cover up," Baxley told the *Birmingham Post-Herald* about the FBI's delay in sharing its evidence. However, once the FBI shared details from its investigation, Baxley was able to file charges against Klansmen Robert E. Chambliss (1904–1985). The key witness against him was Elizabeth Cobbs, Chambliss's niece. In October 1963, she told the FBI about an outburst by Chambliss the day before the bombing and quoted him as saying, "'Let them wait till after Sunday morning. They will beg us to segregate.'" Continuing on, she said that he had commented that he had enough "stuff" to flatten half of Birmingham. Fearing for her own safety, however, she had refused to testify for the FBI in the 1960s. Now, more than a decade later, she was a minister, and she believed it was the only right thing to do. She repeated what she had told the FBI in its original interrogation. On November 18, 1977, Chambliss was convicted of murder and sentenced to life in prison. Chambliss, however, had not acted alone.

HERMAN FRANK CASH (1918–1994) WAS ANOTHER PRIME SUSPECT.

After being convicted of the murder of the four children in the Sixteenth Street Baptist Church dynamite bombing, Thomas Blanton, Jr., was led from the courtroom in handcuffs. The former Ku Klux Klansman was sentenced to life in prison in 2001.

Before Baxley could assemble a case against him, though, Cash died.

Two serious suspects remained: Thomas Blanton, Jr. (1938–), and Bobby Frank Cherry (1930–2004). Both were charged with murder on May 17, 2000. Both proclaimed their innocence. Yet, according to Blanton's FBI lie detector test results from October 1963, it appeared that he had "direct knowledge of and participated . . . in the bombing of the 16th Street Baptist Church." A jury of eight whites and four blacks convicted him of murder in May 2001, and he was led away, hands cuffed in front of him, to spend the remainder of his life in prison.

As for his part, Bobby Frank Cherry, a truck driver and demolitions expert, convicted himself. He used to like to dress up in his Klan robes and dance around in front of his family. After the Sixteenth Street Baptist Church bombing, he boasted to family members and co-workers that he had planted the bomb under the steps at the church. FBI recordings of some of his conversations as well as testimony from family members and former co-workers painted a picture of a hardhearted man who was consumed by racial hatred and violence. When his 2002 verdict came down, the final suspect in the case was convicted of murder and sentenced to life in prison by a jury of his peers—nine whites and three blacks.

Time often changes and heals hearts. Addie Mae's sisters, Janie and Sarah, who lost her right eye in the blast, grew up and married. Both relied on their faith to mend their hearts, but their memories of that Sunday so long ago are frozen in time. Virgil's brother, James, graduated from high school, married, and had two daughters of his own. Sims, filled with remorse for his actions from the start, moved away from Birmingham and married. To pay the debt he felt he owed, he volunteered for the Vietnam War, because he was aware that it was people from poorer families like Virgil's who were being sent to fight. Farley, whose gun was used that fateful September day, was the bitter one in 1963, and his feelings remained unchanged for decades after the incident. He eventually married and had a son. Ironically, he is the one who telephoned James Ware in 1997 to apologize.

In many ways Birmingham changed and healed, also. Out of the rubble of the Sixteenth Street Baptist Church rose a new sanctuary with a stained-glass window donated by the children of Wales in the United Kingdom from money they had saved through a penny campaign. The window features a welcoming black Christ. Kelly Ingram Park is now a landscaped and groomed memorial to the foot soldiers of the children's crusade and to the ministers who led the demonstrations. And across the street from the church is the Birmingham Civil Rights Institute, a museum, an archive, and a reminder that the struggle for civil and human rights in the United States and around the globe still goes on.

For his part in the Sixteenth Street Baptist Church bombing, Bobby Frank Cherry was convicted and sentenced to life in prison. He died in 2004 at the age of seventy-four.

September 15, 1963. Six children died that day— Cynthia, Carole, Addie Mae, Denise, Johnny, and Virgil. Remember them. Their deaths, followed closely by the assassination of President John F. Kennedy, whose administration ushered in civil and voter rights legislation, helped rally support for and spur passage of the reforms of the 1960s. Remember the thirty-nine years it took for justice finally to be served. Remember this, the most horrendous day of the civil rights movement—Birmingham Sunday.

*"You could go in the kitchen and cook their dinner
but you were still not good enough to sit at the table with them."*
—James Ware

FURTHER READING

Bausum, Ann. *Freedom Riders: John Lewis and Jim Zwerg on the Front Lines of the Civil Rights Movement.* Washington, DC: National Geographic Children's Books, 2006.

Brimner, Larry Dane. *We Are One: The Story of Bayard Rustin.* Honesdale, PA: Calkins Creek, 2007.

Collier-Thomas, Bettye, and V. P. Franklin, eds. *Sisters in the Struggle: African American Women in the Civil Rights–Black Power Movement.* New York: New York University Press, 2001.

Curtis, Christopher Paul. *The Watsons Go to Birmingham—1963.* New York: Delacorte Press, 1995.

Fine, Edith Hope. *Rosa Parks: Meet a Civil Rights Hero.* Berkeley Heights, NJ: Enslow, 2004.

Finlayson, Reggie. *We Shall Overcome: The History of the American Civil Rights Movement.* Minneapolis: Lerner Publications, 2003.

Fireside, Harvey. *The "Mississippi Burning" Civil Rights Murder Conspiracy Trial: A Headline Court Case.* Berkeley Heights, NJ: Enslow, 2002.

Freedman, Russell. *Freedom Walkers: The Story of the Montgomery Bus Boycott.* New York: Holiday House, 2006.

———. *The Voice That Challenged a Nation: Marian Anderson and the Struggle for Equal Rights.* New York: Clarion Books, 2004.

Hopkinson, Deborah. *Up Before Daybreak: Cotton and People in America.* New York: Scholastic Nonfiction, 2006.

Landau, Elaine. *The Civil Rights Movement in America: 1954–1968.* New York: Children's Press, 2003.

Levine, Ellen. *Freedom's Children: Young Civil Rights Activists Tell Their Own Stories.* New York: Putnam, 1993.

Mayer, Robert H., ed. *The Civil Rights Act of 1964.* At Issue in History. San Diego: Greenhaven Press, 2004.

Mayer, Robert H. *When the Children Marched: The Birmingham Civil Rights Movement.* Berkeley Heights, NJ: Enslow, 2008.

Meltzer, Milton. *There Comes a Time: The Struggle for Civil Rights.* New York: Random House, 2001.

Miller, Calvin Craig. *No Easy Answers: Bayard Rustin and the Civil Rights Movement.* Greensboro, NC: Morgan Reynolds, 2005.

Olson, Lynne. *Freedom's Daughters: The Unsung Heroines of the Civil Rights Movement from 1830 to 1970.* New York: Scribner, 2001.

Pinkney, Andrea Davis. *Let It Shine: Stories of Black Women Freedom Fighters.* San Diego: Harcourt, 2000.

Waxman, Laura Hamilton. *Coretta Scott King.* Minneapolis: Lerner Publications, 2008.

Weatherford, Carole Boston. *Birmingham, 1963.* Honesdale, PA: Wordsong, 2007.

Whitelaw, Nancy. *Mr. Civil Rights: The Story of Thurgood Marshall.* Greensboro, NC: Morgan Reynolds, 2003.

AUTHOR'S NOTE

I am indebted to those who told Birmingham's story, especially of that tragic Birmingham Sunday, before I did. Newspapers of the time were, of course, valuable sources of information, but articles about the same event often told different accounts depending on their perspective—for instance, whether their readers were African American or white. With this in mind, I read articles in the *Birmingham World*, Birmingham's African American–owned newspaper, before turning to the *Birmingham News* and the *Birmingham Post-Herald*, the city's two leading white-owned publications. Similarly, magazine accounts about an event often differed depending on whether the authors were from the North or from the South. Two articles written by Southern authors long after the events of that Sunday were especially helpful: "Death in the Morning" by Geraldine Watts Bell (*Down Home*, vol. 3, no. 1, Fall 1982, pp. 14–19) and "From Tragedy to Triumph: Honoring Four Little Girls and One Great Woman" by Jaronda Little and Vickii Howell (*Birmingham View,* special commemorative edition published by the Birmingham City Council, October 22, 2005). Several other works were indispensable: *A Fire You Can't Put Out: The Civil Rights Life of Birmingham's Reverend Fred Shuttlesworth* by Andrew M. Manis; *Behind the Stained Glass: A History of Sixteenth Street Baptist Church* by Reverend Dr. Christopher M. Hamlin; *Carry Me Home: Birmingham, Alabama; The Climactic Battle of the Civil Rights Revolution* by Diane McWhorter; *4 Little Girls*, a documentary film by Spike Lee; *Long Time Coming: An Insider's Story of the Birmingham Church Bombing That Rocked the World* by Elizabeth H. Cobbs/Petric J. Smith; and *Until Justice Rolls Down: The Birmingham Church Bombing Case* by Frank Sikora. Other valuable sources included the United States Federal Bureau of Investigation and the Birmingham Police Department surveillance files from the Birmingham Public Library's Department of Archives and Manuscripts. Also critical to my research were the Tenth Judicial Circuit Court trial transcripts of the 1977 trial against Robert E. Chambliss. Finally, the interviews from the Birmingham Civil Rights Institute's Oral History Project, conducted by Dr. Horace Huntley, were invaluable.

ACKNOWLEDGMENTS

The idea for a book about the bombing of the Sixteenth Street Baptist Church and its underlying causes stemmed from a librarians' call for biographies of the four children who were killed on September 15, 1963, which I happened upon in a national publication. When I began my research, I realized that Addie Mae, Cynthia, Carole, and Denise were almost always referred to as "the four little children," "the four little girls," or simply "the four who were killed." Their names seemed almost forgotten to history. Then I realized that they were not the only children killed that day. Two others, Johnny and Virgil, also were victims that Sunday of the hatred that filled Birmingham, Alabama. To write biographies of children so young is an impossible task. They have only begun to experience life. So I decided, instead, to include profiles of them that would hint at their personalities and cloak them within the events of September 15 and the unrest leading up to that horrendous act of terrorism.

With the greatest respect, I referred to African Americans as colored, black, and Negro in this book to be true to the times. These are the terms that African Americans used to refer to themselves and others of their race.

I owe a great thanks to the many people who assisted, encouraged, and supported my efforts. They are Laura Anderson, assistant archivist at the Birmingham Civil Rights Institute; Elizabeth Willauer, librarian, Birmingham Public Library, Southern History Department; James L. Baggett, archivist, Birmingham Public Library, Department of Archives and Manuscripts; Don Veasey, curator of photography, Birmingham Public Library, Department of Archives and Manuscripts; Michelle Andrews, librarian, Birmingham Public Library, Government Documents Department; Peggy Collins, photo editor, Alabama Tourism Department; Voncille Williams, photography technician, the *Birmingham News*; the staff of the Sixteenth Street Baptist Church, who welcomed me; Joan Broerman, author and photo researcher, and her husband, Neal, both of whom kept me housed and fed on numerous trips to Birmingham; Jim Gregg, who made sure that I was at my desk working; Carolyn P. Yoder, Joan Hyman, Jill Goodman, and Tim Gillner, the editorial and design team at Calkins Creek; and finally my mom and dad, both Birmingham natives, for their stories of life in the South.

SOURCE NOTES

Page 6

"Young lady . . . ": Shirley Wesley King, *4 Little Girls*, a documentary film by Spike Lee (New York: 40 Acres and a Mule Filmworks, Inc., 1998).

"It sounded like . . . ": Reverend John H. Cross, "*State of Alabama v. Robert E. Chambliss* Trial," transcript, Department of Archives and Manuscripts, Birmingham Public Library, 1977, p. 64.

Page 8

"deliberate speed": Supreme Court of the United States in *Brown v. Board of Education of Topeka*, syllabus, Legal Information Institute, Supreme Court Collection, Cornell University Law School, www.law.cornell.edu/supct/html/historics/USSC_CR_0349_0294_ZS.html, p. 1 (accessed June 22, 2008).

Page 9

"Segregation today . . . ": George C. Wallace, "The 1963 Inaugural Address of Governor George C. Wallace," transcript, Alabama Department of Archives and History, www.archives.state.al.us/govs_list/inauguralspeech.html, p. 3 (accessed March 31, 2008).

Page 12

"the biggest thing . . . ": Fred Shuttlesworth, interview by Horace B. Huntley, Ph.D., December 10, 1996, *Oral History Project*, transcript (tape 3), Birmingham Civil Rights Institute, p. 1.

"resulted in hardening . . . ": Ibid.

Page 15

"You may knock me down . . . ": song, "I Am Free," negrospirituals.com, www.negrospirituals.com/news-song/i_am_free.htm (accessed April 5, 2008).

"Well . . . ": Shuttlesworth, *Oral History Project*, p. 28.

Page 16

"We want no cowards . . . ": song, "Children, We All Shall Be Free," www.negrospirituals.com, www.negrospirituals.com/news-song/children_we_all_shall_be_free.htm (accessed April 5, 2008).

"the Negro feared most . . . ": Howard K. Smith, "Who Speaks for Birmingham?," transcript, *CBS Reports*, produced by Fred W. Friendly and David Lowe (New York: Columbia Broadcasting System, Inc., 1961).

Page 21

"We shall overcome . . . ": song, "We Shall Overcome," negrospirituals.com, www.negrospirituals.com/news-song/we_shall_overcome.htm (accessed April 5, 2008).

Page 32

"it was making it . . . ": Reverend John H. Cross, interview by Horace B. Huntley, Ph.D., July 27, 1997, *Oral History Project*, transcript, Birmingham Civil Rights Institute, p. 20.

"started telling people . . . ": Ibid.

"be brought . . . ": Ibid.

"This was . . . ": Ibid.

"[T]hey were all . . . ": Ibid.

"Bomb Blast . . . ": "Bomb Blast Kills 4 Children, Injures 17 at Church Here," headline, *Birmingham Post-Herald*, September 16, 1963, Department of Archives and Manuscripts, Birmingham Public Library.

Page 33

"On Birmingham Sunday . . . ": song, "Birmingham Sunday," words by Richard Fariña. San Francisco: Bread and Roses Benefit Agency, 1964.

Page 34

"She would have . . . ": Gerald Colbert, *4 Little Girls*.

"She was caring . . . ": Dr. Freeman Hrabowski, III, *4 Little Girls*.

Page 35

"Carole was a . . . ": Carolyn Lee Brown, *4 Little Girls*.

"She played clarinet . . . ": Alpha Robertson, *4 Little Girls*.

Page 36

"To know Addie . . . ": Janie Gaines, *4 Little Girls*.

"She was just . . . ": Ibid.

Page 37

"'You're not too . . . '": Maxine McNair, *4 Little Girls*.

Page 39

"No we didn't . . . ": James Ware, interview by Horace B. Huntley, Ph.D., September 17, 1997, *Oral History Project*, transcript, Birmingham Civil Rights Institute, p. 5.

"[W]ow . . . ": Ibid.

Page 40

"Well, it wasn't . . . ": James Ware, interview by Horace B. Huntley, Ph.D., September 17, 1997, *Oral History Project*, transcript, Birmingham Civil Rights Institute, p. 5.

"To tell you . . . ": Ibid.

"We certainly beat . . . ": Governor George C. Wallace, "We Got Jump on Kennedy Crowd, Governor Says," by Hugh W. Sparrow, *Birmingham News*, October 1, 1963, p. 1.

Page 43

"I am not so . . . ": William J. Baxley, "Baxley: Justice Dept. Slowed Bombing Probe," UPI, *Birmingham Post-Herald*, November 30, 1977, p. D3.

"Let them wait . . . ": Elizabeth Cobbs, "United States Federal Bureau of Investigation Sixteenth Street Baptist Church Bombing Investigation Files," report by Special Agent Robert P. Womack, October 12, 1963. Department of Archives and Manuscripts, Birmingham Public Library, File # 1308.1.8.

"stuff ": Ibid.

Page 44

"direct knowledge of . . . ": Special Agent F. Willard Ralston, "United States Federal Bureau of Investigation Sixteenth Street Baptist Church Bombing Investigation Files," polygraph interview, October 1, 1963. Department of Archives and Manuscripts, Birmingham Public Library, File # 1308.2.7, p. Y.

Page 46

"You could go . . . ": Ware, *Oral History Project*, p. 8.

PICTURE CREDITS

Birmingham

BIRMINGHAM: Cloudy, mild, showers.

Alabama's 'Good Mor

VOL. 93—NO. 163

BIRMINGHAM, MONDAY

BOMB BLASTS
STATE TROOPER